Tony was born in Dublin Ireland, and has lived there all his life. Uneducated he worked at manual labour up to his sixties. In his sixties he decided to go to adult education, at Saoir-Ollscoil na hÉireann, free University of Ireland, were he went on to receive a BA degree in Liberal Arts. Tony's reasons for this booklet, is to help and impower anyone who may be unhappy with a relationship, with themselves, suffering from unexplained illness, or perhaps life in general.

Tony Jennings

TONY'S CHOICE

AUSTIN MACAULEY PUBLISHERS™
LONDON • CAMBRIDGE • NEW YORK • SHARJAH

Copyright © Tony Jennings 2023

The right of Tony Jennings to be identified as author of this work has been asserted by the author in accordance with sections 77 and 78 of the Copyright, Designs and Patents Act 1988.

All rights reserved. No part of this publication may be reproduced, stored in a retrieval system, or transmitted in any form or by any means, electronic, mechanical, photocopying, recording, or otherwise, without the prior permission of the publishers.

Any person who commits any unauthorised act in relation to this publication may be liable to criminal prosecution and civil claims for damages.

All of the events in this memoir are true to the best of the author's memory. The views expressed in this memoir are solely those of the author.

A CIP catalogue record for this title is available from the British Library.

ISBN 9781035803835 (Paperback)
ISBN 9781035803842 (ePub e-book)

www.austinmacauley.com

First Published 2023
Austin Macauley Publishers Ltd®
1 Canada Square
Canary Wharf
London
E14 5AA

A very special thanks to Sister Basil Gaffney, without her unending patience, help and encouragement this would not be possible, and thanks also to Mairéad Ni Chíosóig and Saor-Ollscoil na hÉireann for her support and the use of the library.

I was born in Dublin in 1953; the eldest of five to a working-class family. My childhood years were traumatic; my father was alcoholic and violence in the home was frequent. This had a profound effect on me as a child; my memories of my school days are very confused. I was unaware of it at the time, but throughout my entire life, I have suffered with anxiety. Because of this, my concentration in school was zero, and I felt that I was no good at anything. At that period in my life, school was a punishment; believing that I was no good at anything and trying to do the small bit of homework I got, was impossible. My young life was very simplistic; do not ask questions and do what you are told. At 12 years of age, I left school and started a lifetime of manual labour. Going through life without education was extremely difficult; the obstacles are too numerous to mention. I married at 20 and my wife gave birth to our first child, a boy, in 1975 and our second child, a boy, was born in 1979. The two boys are a tonic.

At a late stage in my life, I received a flyer in the letter box; it offered an opportunity to study for a BA degree in liberal arts for mature adults from Saor-Ollscoil na hÉireann (Free University of Ireland). This got into my subconscious, and as the days passed, I became more and more interested. Having no formal education, it was very difficult for me to take the first step; I had no confidence. But deep down, this was something I wanted, just for myself, just to feel good about myself. So, I got the courage to go in that door and make inquiries; this was extremely difficult for me. Not having confidence in oneself affects almost everything you do. Just to be able to articulate your opinion in a work situation is impossible. As a result, you do what you are told and go through life frustrated. I have worked with people with little or no education, and others with education, some with confidence and others not. I soon realised that for those with confidence, life was a lot easier.

Upon entering the door of Saor-Ollscoil na hÉireann, I was greeted by a lady who introduced herself as Mairéad. I started the conversation by referring to the flyer I had with me, and to the reservations I felt regarding my suitability. From the very start, Mairéad made me feel comfortable. She smiled and said, "The only requirement is a love of learning." This feeling I was experiencing was overwhelming; for the first time in my life I felt a complete person. Mairéad went on to explain, "The BA degree in liberal arts is awarded on a basis of a minimum of 50 credits between course work and a thesis. The student aims to accumulate 25 or more credits from course work over a minimum of three years. Credits are also awarded for presentations made, attendance at seminars, field trips and summer schools. The university is a free and independent institute, and all the lecturers and administrators give their time free of charge."

I would strongly encourage any person who has no confidence in themselves not to leave working towards gaining confidence too late in life, as I have done. Make the choice to do something about it. You are a human being; each person in this world is special. You are no less a person than the leader of your country or the pope. Choose to go to classes; perhaps assertiveness classes; public speaking classes; joining a choir is excellent; singing in a group gives a person confidence plus the added bonus of interacting with others. I would encourage anybody suffering from a sense of inferiority to choose to say to yourself, "I am no different from anyone else. I can choose to go through life feeling like this or I can choose to do something about it."

The first year was strange. Getting to know my strengths and weaknesses was difficult; most things went over my head. The second year, I began to settle down. I was starting to feel comfortable. I was feeling good about myself; my confidence was building. It was around this time that I decided psychology interested me the most. The following year, a new tutor arrived for psychology, Sister Basil Gaffney. Sister Basil introduced choice theory psychology to the class. Choice theory psychology, also known as Glaserian psychology, is the psychology of a world-renowned 20th century psychologist, Dr William Glasser (1925–2013). Choice theory psychology emphasises a person's control over his or her own feelings and actions and teaches the concept that all behaviour is chosen in order to satisfy each person's five basic needs which are love and belonging, power, freedom, fun and survival.

One of the first things Sister Basil asked the class was, "If you are driving a car and you come up to a red traffic light, do you have to stop?"

I, for one, said, "Yes."

Sister Basil said, "You do not have to stop, rather you choose to stop." I was fascinated by this response. I went on to learn that all anyone or anything outside of us can do is give us information. Bells, buzzers, lights, and whistles give information; it is a person's choice to heed them or not. Human beings are internally motivated. No person is a stimulus – response system that stops, for example when a light turns red or answers a phone because it rings. A person chooses a behaviour to satisfy a need. At that time in my life, my answer to a lot of situations was what choice do I have. Looking back now, a lot of my responses were just a type of language I had picked up growing up. Now I have become very aware of people's responses to a lot of things, and it is amazing how often I hear, 'what choice do I have'.

Unless someone is holding a gun to you, or you are in a prison situation, you always have a choice. It may not be a great choice, or the best choice, but most of the time we have choices, and sometimes choosing a different behaviour works out for the better. When you come to realise this, you start making better choices about your life.

Without realising it, a person's behaviour can cause all sorts of problems including feeling unwell. We tend to blame others for our misery – "You're driving me crazy" – without realising our thoughts are our choice. Choice theory develops a sense of internal control, self-direction, independence, and high self-esteem, thus empowering a person to take responsibility for their chosen behaviours. Becoming aware of this for the first time can be empowering. Realising that what you do is internally motivated. In other words, it is you and only you, who has chosen to behave in whatever way you do. It gives you a great feeling, a feeling of control over your life; now you are the driver of your destiny. I would suggest testing it out. The next time you get annoyed, say to yourself, "I wonder if I choose to stop being annoyed will it work." Or perhaps you might choose to change a behaviour that has become part of your life and you really don't like it. It could be always finding fault with others; it could be meanness; you could choose to be a little more generous; it could be laziness; you could choose to help out more in the home. It may be overeating. This behaviour, you may in fact know, is not good for you. You could choose to change that behaviour. Whenever you think about overeating, say to yourself, "No, this behaviour is bad for me."

People choose to change behaviours all the time without realising or appreciating the fact that this is a power they have within themselves. We say, "I have changed my mind" if it is something important to a person. This change of mind indicates the freedom a person has to choose differently. We can make a choice to change our mind. When it is important, there is no hesitation about choosing what feels good or what, we hope, may turn out better. Choosing to go or not to go on holiday, choosing to work overtime, choosing not to work, choosing to say to yourself, "I am in a bad mood", choosing to say, "I feel great. I would love to go dancing", choosing not to eat that cream cake. All our behaviours are our choices; they are our responses to fulfilling our needs and wants in the world in which we live. Positive choices have the ability to turn a person's life around for the better. By getting a proper balance – physically and mentally – a person starts to discover who he or she really is as a person; life becomes meaningful and fulfilling.

The purpose of this booklet is to try to help anybody who is suffering in any way. Suffering can be unexplained headaches, fatigue, frustration, unhappiness, loneliness, low self-esteem, depression, bad temper, intimidation, or bullying.

We all need meaning in our lives. The absence of a super being, call him or her God if you like, makes a person's life empty and meaningless. In the last 80 years, the speed at which science and technology have advanced is mind blowing. Every year it is getting faster, coupled with the fact that we are chattels to a tiny elite who play with the global economy. This contributes to confusion and stress. There is no denying, advancements are of great benefit to mankind, especially when you think of medical procedures. Technology is changing people's behaviours; the use of technology is now part of life. Unfortunately, many young people are spending far too much time looking at screens; this overuse is depriving them of personal interaction and socialising with their peers. Personal contact with others helps young people discover who they are, their likes and dislikes. An example of this technology would be a mobile phone. It is of fantastic benefit for some but for others it has become an obsession; it is almost perceived as in the same context for survival as the need for food. Unable to function without it, panic sets in if they break it, lose it, or even, forget it.

Difficulties and problems that people experience through their lives have not changed much over time. Older people were able, in a lot of cases, to identify such problems and help relatives and friends. This culture is the same worldwide. It is important that young people engage in their communities, getting involved in one way or another, to ensure that thousands of years of knowledge and the culture of today will survive and continue to evolve.

If information and perspective are obtained only through a screen, dealing with the real world will be difficult if not impossible. Violence has increased considerably in recent years. A reason for this could be that due to the fact that some young people viewing and playing aggressive video games confuse what they see on a screen with reality. When a person is communicating and interacting with others, they learn some of life skills; if, for example, someone offends or assaults them, they instantly know what it is like to be offended or hurt, not the world of fantasy observed from a screen. The conversations a six to ten-year-old has with their peers are part of the foundations in the formation of the child's personality. They are learning from each other; their strengths and weaknesses, their likes and dislikes. The young person that spends excessive amount of time in their room looking at a computer is not engaging with reality, and is depriving themselves of family experience, intimacy, and personal interaction.

Throughout history, people have contributed creatively to society. There were creative people who had the eagerness and the ability to work with their hands, as carpenters, stonemasons, electricians, painters, mechanics, artists, and musicians. If people are not engaging with reality but are living their life in a fantasy world, society will break down. People need to interact with each other there is no replacement for personal contact. Sexual attraction is a frequent topic of discussion among men and woman, and this is commendable as young people need to talk about their feelings with their peers. A young person who has spent all their spare time looking at a screen does not have any idea how to behave when socialising with others. When the only companion a person has is a screen, trying to deal with the problems in life that sometimes come up to bite you can be very difficult; this could result in loneliness and such people seeking refuge in drugs or alcohol.

The following is an article from https://www.thejournal.ie 14/6/2019, written by, Laoighseach Ní Choistealbha, an Irish Research Council Laureate on the project 'Republic of Conscience: Human Rights and Modern Irish Poetry in NUI Galway'.

Opinion: Quitting Social Media Enriched My Life Hugely – Would You Dare to Hit Delete?

OVER CHRISTMAS 2018 I posted a status on Facebook announcing that I was leaving the site. I was fully in the network. I scrolled, liked, shared, and commented, I engaged in all of the etiquette required of modern relationships. I had more than a thousand friends. My statuses and photo uploads earned me hearts, comments, likes, and reshares. I had created and maintained 'friendships' on the site which I saw as the beating heart of my social life, connecting me to the lives of my friends through a web of online engagement, news, icons, likes and clicks. I had set up my Facebook account in the year 2009 when I was fifteen. The Internet didn't mean much to me at the time though, we didn't have an internet connection at home until 2007, so while my pre-Facebook years were spent posting embarrassing comments on Bebo and arranging my Top 16 friends with care – I was more interested in reading, art, and schoolwork.

Building Up Your Profile.

But then in time, as Facebook outlasted Bebo, my classmates were joined on the online hub by Gaeltacht acquaintances, school mates that I hardly knew, who were in turn followed by college friends and strangers that I met in a nightclub bathroom. "I'll add you on Facebook! We should definitely meet up!" We promised. Facebook was part of life, part of us. We were our online personae, and those artificial personae were us: an ersatz mirror-image of ourselves. Potential friends or lovers would scan over our Facebook pages like a kind of baseline curriculum vitae of our lives. We fussed over our profiles, touched them up and built up our online selves over years and decades.

I once met someone my own age who didn't have social media at all, and I was shocked. I backed away from him subconsciously; this modern-day Luddite who eschewed what made the rest of us normal, connected, together. Who didn't want to be part of that collective? Who didn't want to construct their own personality shrine to present to the world? I eyed him suspiciously, from the safety of the connected tribe.

Who cares?

When I posted a status announcing that I was leaving Facebook, no one cared. We delude ourselves into this fantasy of connection, that these sites help us maintain friendship and connect with people. Over a decade of having a Facebook account, I had connected with more than a thousand people, and I imagined that my sudden exit from the site would provoke a reaction with a slew of people begging me to stay. Of course, none of them did. I mentioned in my status that anyone who wanted to connect with me should request my email or phone number, expecting hoards to descend upon me in a panic. Roughly ten people messaged me requesting my contact details, which is about 1% of my Facebook 'friends'. And those were all people that I knew well in real life, they were close friends and acquaintances with whom most of my dealings were already happening offline.

The fact that no one cared I was leaving Facebook was both saddening and liberating. It was saddening in the sense that I had spent hours maintaining an online presence for people who didn't care if they never saw my carefully chosen profile picture again; it was liberating in the sense that I had now chosen a life that would not have the background chatter of people with whom I hadn't spoken in years and that I no longer had to worry about their disinterested gaze on my life.

But Facebook doesn't make it easy to leave.

Quitting is never easy.

First, you have to deactivate the account, and then delete it. There's no well-signposted way of removing yourself from their service. I had to search online for how to complete the task, as I couldn't find the delete function. Once I had managed to complete the necessary steps, however, Facebook hit me with some emotional blackmail. It brought up a page with the faces of my most engaged with Facebook friends: my mother, my brother, my partner, my friends. Facebook asked me if I was sure that I wanted to leave my connections with all of these people. The sight of that page made me feel bad. Briefly, I doubted my decision, thinking these are my friends and I'm withdrawing from them. I'm betraying our connection. Then, I remembered the only 1% of my Facebook friends actually cared enough to ask for my email and I firmly clicked the final deletion button and just like that, the persona that I had maintained with care and attention for almost a decade, disappeared. So, fall the dominoes.

With Facebook gone, the other social media sites fell away; Instagram, Snapchat, and Twitter were deleted by April 2019, almost without a thought (although I retained LinkedIn for professional purposes). They meant nothing.

My days became longer. My tasks became completed. My life became streamlined. My work became more productive. My friends became real.

I grieved for the thousands of hours I had spent online that I could never get back, squandered on the architecture of nothingness. I woke up and didn't check my phone. I called people. I met people. I deleted the email apps from my phone. I turned my phone off during work hours. I checked email on my desktop computer once a day. I wrote most of a poetry collection. I went to yoga classes, and I lost 42 pounds (I had been seriously overweight). I began to live an analogue life, as much as possible. I became an analogue millennial.

I respect technology and all that it does for us. But I understand now how much it demands from us in return.

One evening, as I went out for a stroll enjoying the April air, I walked past a gourmet burger restaurant in Galway city centre. I glanced in the window of the restaurant: a family of six, circled around a table, five of them staring downwards at their mobile phones. The oldest family member (either a father, uncle, or grandfather) was gazing out of the window as I passed. Our eyes met.

Science and technology have side effects on everybody. The number of people with mental health problems just keeps rising and this is a concern asking the question, why are so many people committing suicide? This fast-moving ever-changing world can be difficult for a large number of people. There are all types of excellent groups being formed to help people, but we are not asking the question, 'Why is it this generation has almost every conceivable mental health issue?' There are some who would say, "But back then we had nothing." While acknowledging that problems were there in the past, I would say we had contentment and peace of mind; we had time to think, to discover ourselves, to dream, time to talk to our neighbours and friends, time to read a book or just fall asleep if we felt like it. When the majority of the population were poor, there was no stigma attached to anyone. They all had nothing. There were no designer labels, wearing second-hand clothes was normal. Poor people would share food with their neighbours. Then along came the rich person who wanted more riches and gave us all credit. This in some respects is helpful, until you are unable to repay this loan; now that poor person is even poorer. This style of credit has become normalised with many. It is unhealthy; it has become a constant source of worry for the youth of today. The rich have capitalised on this and given us ratings. So now our value as a person is down to how good or bad our credit ratings are.

The availability of antidepressants, alcohol and escape routes has become a global epidemic. We need a balance to our lives; mind and body are not in harmony if you have to take drugs. Regardless of what anyone tells you, we need to slow down. We used to walk through life, now we run, and that makes it hard to be on our guard against destructive elements. Or it could lead to people losing interest in a meaningful life and they could become complacent especially as they grow older. Choosing to change habits can help. Most people tend to repeat a lot of things. For example, I keep going to the same barber; not that there is anything wrong with that, but as we get older, we are inclined to keep doing the same things over and over. A lot of people spend excessive amount of their time sitting watching television; some of that time could be used to exercise or to get involved in a local group.

There is nothing more important than your health. You are no good to anyone without your health, not yourself, your family, your job. The number of people with health problems is phenomenal, many have problems that cannot be explained. In a large amount of cases, doctors can find no pathology, no reason why the person is suffering the way there are.

Whenever we decide to do something, business, sport, or leisure, we plan; and the best plan has a system. We need a system in life in order to reach our ultimate goal. Choice theory is one such system that gives us the freedom to choose a pathway to God and self-fulfilment. God has given us the freedom of choice; we all make good and bad choices throughout our lives. Choosing to have God in our life can only be good. Evil is all around us; we have a constant battle with evil. If you accept that good exists, then the opposite is true. Unfortunately, it is part of life. Unkind thoughts constantly challenge us. It is when we entertain them, they grow and fester. There are many examples of evil that have become an everyday occurrence. A paedophile is a person who has allowed evil to infiltrate their mind, and when an evil thought possess the mind, cruel, immoral, criminal acts or violent sexual acts is the likely result. Terrorism all over the world is another example of what happens when we allow evil thoughts such as greed or hatred of other people dominate our mind. War crimes are an act of evil. Our natural God-given feelings for others is lost. Modern day slavery, where advantage is taken of vulnerable human beings, can only be described as wicked and criminal. Young people with their young impressionable minds watching all types of violence on television or media get warped; they become desensitised and their attitude to life can become affected. There is so much violence that it has become normalised. Political and large corporate decisions that inflict hardship on the masses is evil. Whenever we entertain evil thoughts, we become blind to reality; we lose our natural gift of feeling that God has given us. This consciousness of good and bad is our guide through life. Evil can be cancerous. It can eat you up resulting in you living a life of criticising, punishing, blaming, and threatening.

The following scripture passage are from Ephesians 6: 10–17 are encouraging:

"Grow strong in the lord with the strength of his power. Put on the full armour of God so as to be able to resist the devil's tactics. For it is not against human enemies that we have to struggle, but against the principalities and the ruling forces who are masters of the darkness in this world, the spirits of evil in the heavens. That is why you must take up all God's armour, or you will not be able to put up any resistance on the evil day, or stand your ground even though you exert yourself to the full. So stand your ground, with truth a belt round your waist, and uprightness a breastplate, wearing for shoes on your feet the eagerness to spread the gospel of peace and always carrying the shield of faith so that you can use it to quench the burning arrows of the Evil One. And then you must take salvation as your helmet and the sword of the spirit, that is, the word of God."

This wisdom from the scriptures guides informs and enables us to make the right choices. For a moment, contemplate how wonderful life would be, if going through life God's commandments were observed. Our lives would be free from all the negatives that society has created. What the children of the present, and fearfully, the children of the future are exposed to, is driven by consumerism. Many young people are born into a lifestyle of consumerism, brainwashed into making choices that have no foundation, no relevance to living a satisfying, good, and meaningful life. Young people are being presented with a lifestyle that only a very small percentage can achieve or afford, and this lifestyle has no foundation. In my opinion, the biggest contributor to this way of life is credit. Before credit, we all lived according to our means. Most people who hunger for this way of life, and eventually enter this world of consumerism, end up sad, empty, lonely people, appreciating few of life's values. No person should feel insecure or have to go through life in fear, or burdened with anxiety, confused, and forever questioning their choices, wondering are they right. We are all God's children, regardless of shape, size, colour, disability. Jesus was the first person to introduce equality; he reached out to all, told them they were not servants of masters, rather that they were children of God. Jesus gave them positive energy, a belief that each person was equal, he gave them a feeling or sense of independence. Before Jesus came on earth, people were suppressed from thousands of years of bondage and slavery. Jesus gave people a sense of their uniqueness, belonging and freedom. This gave people positive energy, light and hope for the future; they were able to explore, make decisions and improve their way of life.

God loves everyone equally; when He chose Moses, it did not concern Him that he had a speech impediment. This choice was one of the most significant choices in the history of mankind. Of all the people He had to choose from, He chose a person with a speech impediment. Society has a responsibility to care for the vulnerable among us, for we know not when we will join them. Not to do so is neglecting our responsibility as human beings. Such neglected behaviour means giving up on love. Jesus, in his day, admonished the inhabitants of Jerusalem for their treatment of the prophets and those who are different.

"Jerusalem, Jerusalem, you that kill the prophets and stone those who are sent to you! How often have I longed to gather your children together, as a hen gathers her chicks under her wings, and you refused! Look! Your house will be deserted, for, I promise, you shall not see me anymore until you are saying: Blessed is he who is coming in the name of the lord!" Matthew 23:37.

I have come across a number of people who are unsure as to the choices they should make for their life in order to lead fulfilling satisfying lives. Perhaps people might give thought to questions such as: "What would I really like to do with my life?"; "What could I do that is productive and makes me feel good?"; "What gift has God given me to share with others?" Giving is receiving; when we give to the world, our community, our neighbour, we receive a feeling no money can buy, this feeling is the harmony of mind and body. Most of us remember times in our life when things were going right and how good we felt. By sharing some of our time, we contribute to the happiness of others. When mind and body are in harmony, we are happy and content as human beings. At present, some are forgetting the pleasures we once had, before commercialism, when we had very little, the fun and joy that we found in the simplest of things. Listening to our elders and the wisdom they have can be very beneficial, both for young and old. There is so much knowledge from the past that has been lost. We are where we are because of the past. We stand on the shoulders of previous generations.

The family is so important; choosing to maintain good communication with everyone in the family circle ensures positive relationships. The family unit is an integral part of life. For the majority, this is where our need for love and belonging is satisfied. This love and belonging are the fuel of life. It is the foundation of life and is one of our basic needs in order to live a satisfying and balanced life. In the knowledge that somebody cares, our lives are made more meaningful. It is to the family we return at the end of the day. The family is where we grow, and learn to give and take; a place to share our joys and disappointments, but unfortunately, we can often take it for granted because it is so much part of us. Jesus knew the dynamics of family life; he was part of a family. Growing up he would have witnessed all the trials and tribulations that his mother and foster father endured. God's love for the family is unending.

The knowledge and practice of choice theory psychology enabled me to listen and think differently. Knowing we have five basic needs – survival, love and belonging, fun, freedom, and power – that motivate us to behave. Hunger is top of our survival need, in order to meet that need, we eat and drink; our love and belonging need will make us show affection for the people in our lives whom we care about. The things we want in life are always pleasurable. We always try our best when choosing a behaviour that it feels good. We do not choose behaviours that feel bad or painful. Some people may find folding and ironing clothes extremely cumbersome and avoid it, whereas some will find it pleasurable and enjoy the exercise. Therefore, we avoid behaviours that do not feel pleasurable.

We also have what Glasser describes as a quality world; this quality world starts from the time we are born. It consists of memories or pictures of people, places and things that are stored in our quality world of the things that please us. We visit this vast array of pictures in our mind on a regular basis, and this exercise prompts us to behave in such a way as to satisfy whatever picture we want to satisfy a particular need. This may be a holiday you enjoyed as a child, or it could be some type of food, or possibly a particular type of car. Whatever the want is, our quality world prompts us to behave in order to satisfy the need based on the picture in our mind or quality world.

This new approach, the choice theory approach, to everyday occurrences was uplifting for me; it gave me a freedom I could never have imagined. I was able to look at situations differently, relationships were better, my self-esteem was growing, my road rage stopped. I realised that such behaviour was a bad choice. As already stated, choice theory informs us that we choose all behaviours. Our motivation for all our behaviour is internal. Therefore, we cannot say, "He or she made me do it." People choose behaviours for various reasons; each choice is a personal choice. As one begins to make better choices, the act of doing so becomes easier and eventually, one hopes, automatic. I expect there are people like me who for one reason or another find themselves at a loose end, a bit confused about what direction to take in life asking the question what is it all about.

I would recommend reading and reflecting on choice theory, and talking to your higher power, and hopefully you will find courage and consolation.

Choice theory psychology provides an effective model of behaviour for living a satisfactory life. It is a liberating, empowering psychology that reveals a power and a faith within each person which makes it possible for them to choose behaviours that will change their lives for the better. It enables a person to take control of their own destiny. We make hundreds of choices every day without thinking about them. Whenever we make a choice, at that precise moment, it is our best choice. In the eyes of others, or objectively speaking, it may be a bad choice, but it is our best choice. If you go shopping for a pair of shoes, the shoes you buy will be your best choice, otherwise you would have picked a different pair. A month or six months later, you may not like them, but at that precise moment, it was your best choice.

When it comes to the more important issues in life, of interacting with people, our best choice can be improved with the help of choice theory. Choice theory advocates that each person cultivate the connecting habits recommended by William Glasser which are: listing, respecting, accepting, encouraging, supporting, trusting, and negotiating. Understanding this can help some of us who for one reason or another, find it difficult to accept some of our past choices. I regret a lot of my past choices, but with this new knowledge of choice theory, I know I cannot change the past, but I can plan for the future. Now, together with awareness of choice theory, and my belief in the constant presence of God, I strive to make the best possible choices that I can in my life. We all have the ability to bring happiness, satisfaction and self-fulfilment to our lives, and the lives of others, by the choices we make in our daily lives. If you have been suffering in any way, and the behaviour you have chosen has not satisfied your needs you might try and be more creative in your choice of behaviour. For example, not wanting to talk to people in general, not wanting to go outside, feeling overwhelmed about everything, being fearful of crowds, having panic attacks, whatever the problem is, take some time each day to pray, ask for help. Say to yourself, "I know that what I am now doing is not enabling me to live a full life, so now I need to choose a different way of life." The power of prayer is limitless; ask God to give you the strength to choose a new behaviour. Look at how you might change your behaviour, just a small change, slowly, gradually, and you will, hopefully, overcome whatever problems there are. Remember, this time you will have a very close friend with you, so trust in God and yourself.

From my studies in choice theory, I felt a freedom and confidence and a great sense of contentment. I was able to accept my life and find enjoyment, and at the same time, make efforts to improve it. I found that once you come to accept your situation in life, in most cases, it starts to get better. For example, try not to complain about things in general and you will find the things you were complaining about have no real importance in life anymore. Before my introduction to choice theory, I was just drifting through life, no direction, always complaining and moaning about something, endless bouts of frustration, not knowing why I felt the way I did; the knowledge of choice theory psychology has changed all that.

Dr Glasser talks about the seven habits that we should avoid because they isolate us from meaningful relationships in our very small world. Knowing them now helps me see why I was so frustrated in the past. Three of the seven habits that affected me most were complaining, blaming, and criticising because they reduced my ability to mature. The other four deadly divisive habits are nagging, threatening, punishing, rewarding to control. I know now from experience that my choosing the seven caring connecting habits of choice theory – listening, respecting, accepting, encouraging, supporting, trusting, and negotiating – I can see things differently and my life is more enjoyable.

Understanding why we do what we do, and why we feel what we feel, opened a whole new world for me. It enabled me to take control of my life. Choice theory explains that we are all motivated by pleasure which, in practice, means that whether or not we feel pain, we always want to learn how to behave in order to feel better. And all pleasure and pain are derived from our efforts to satisfy the five basic needs of survival, love and belonging, power, freedom, and fun which we are born with. All behaviour that satisfies one or more of these needs is pleasurable. All behaviour that attempts, but fails, to satisfy one or more of these needs is painful. The strength of the needs varies enormously. The fun-need is enjoyment and learning; a person with a high fun-need will always want to learn new things and will always enjoy socialising. The freedom-need is the opportunity to choose among various possibilities and to act on our own without unreasonable restraints. A person with a high freedom-need would prefer to be self-employed. The power-need is to seek achievement, competence, and accomplishment and the need to feel inner and external control of our lives. A person with a high power-need may look for a career in politics or show-business.

This understanding enabled me to take control of my life. Choice theory allowed me to choose the life I wanted to live. Now, I am dealing with the world more effectively. I am seeing things differently; I realise that a lot of my anxiety was because of my high freedom-need. I also discovered why some people never travel, but at the same time are happy and content, because their freedom-need is low. It was like I had just been given permission to live a free life, and to choose whatever effort that was needed to meet my basic needs. Like me, I am sure there are a lot of people who suffer with no confidence, thinking they may be different in some way. Choice theory enables us to understand that we are all different. Understanding that there are vast differences in the strengths of people's needs and how each person lives their life through their quality world will restore their confidence. This quality world is a vast collection of our likes and aspirations we have logged in our brain from the time we are born. Education is a powerful thing; every person on this earth has the ability to further their education provided they are interested in the subject chosen.

My newfound contentment started a line of thought in me; this embraced a higher power. Looking back on my life, I was never really with God. When I think of all the situations and predicaments that I have had over the course of my life, some that were life threatening. Now that I have found God, I find myself thinking how much easier life could have been had I come to find him early. In the early days of getting to know him, I found talking to God strange. As the weeks and months passed, I found it very comforting talking to God; now I have a real meaning in and of life.

In the past, whenever I had to go somewhere strange, I sometimes felt fearful. Now I say to myself, "I have nothing to fear anymore. I have God with me." This works for me; it gives strength and courage and for me it works. My personality has changed. I am more approachable; strangers stop to talk to me, whereas before, I obviously must have been displaying some negativity. After my study research and subsequently my practice in using choice theory, I also found that if you embrace this psychology, and work at making better choices, the results you get are positive. I believe there is a higher power motivating us should we choose to respond to the inspiration.

Understanding why we behave is like solving a puzzle; you have that 'now I get it moment' and with that feeling or information you can start choosing behaviours that are satisfying; behaviours that balance the natural harmony of mind and body. Most of us are aware of situations that have made us feel uncomfortable as a result of a chosen behaviour. By observing situations, considering different behaviours, better choices can present themselves. So by making better choices and choosing different behaviours, we can restore harmony and balance to mind and body; this is paramount for happiness. Getting your mind and body in harmony is so important; by making better choices you can achieve this. For example, some people may always end up arguing with a particular person whenever they meet. With the knowledge of choice theory, they can choose a new behaviour and make a conscious choice not to say or do anything that would facilitate an argument. In other words, use the connecting habits and avoid the disconnecting ones. It could happen that a work-related behaviour or a family incident leaves you feeling uncomfortable, by choosing to change that behaviour you can restore harmony. It could be that you know you could do better in a particular situation, but you choose not to bother. That is a choice you make. How each person conducts their life is a personal thing, therefore, it's a wise thing that each one of us examine our behaviour in our daily struggle for contentment. We have all witnessed unacceptable behaviour from people in everyday life; behaviour we may not agree with, but we do not know how we would behave if we found ourselves in their situation. People can be their own worst enemy because of their behaviour. Choice theory can enable us to choose behaviours that will contribute to our peace of mind.

I have been using this word 'choice' all my life in a meaningless sort of way, sort of like the way some people use the word actually; we tend to throw it out there, without any thought about what we are saying. Most of us find ourselves saying, "I have to do this" or "I have to go there" or "What choice do I have?" or "We do not have to do anything we do not want to do." Some people in the world choose a lifestyle of non-conformity with accepted norms of the jurisdiction in which they find themselves. Most of the things that we find cumbersome to do, in fact, we have chosen to do.

Taking care of a sick family member can be stressful, but in most cases, we choose this out of love. It would be difficult to get people to work if there was no financial reward. Therefore, we choose to work for the reward. We say things like "I have to go to work", or "I have to cook the dinner"; we do not have to do such things we choose to do them. You may say, "If I did not go to work, I would starve", and you would probably be right, but you could also choose to starve. I know this is an extreme example; I am just trying to get my point across that things are not black and white. Most of the times, there are alternatives. I find the theory of choice which states that you do not have to do something if you choose not to, makes doing what I do a whole lot easier, in the knowledge that what I am doing is my choice. Understandably, without knowing choice theory, we think other people are making us make some of our choices. When we come to realise that every thought, and physical action is our choice, it is freeing. This means that nobody makes us do anything, everything we do is our choice. With this information, and knowing you are in control, you can choose to change a behaviour you may not like about yourself.

For me, this word, 'choice' is a game changer. The small acorn has the ability to produce a massive oak tree. The transformation that this small word 'choice' can have on a person's life has to be a gift from God. I would encourage everyone to use this gift of choice, and have faith in whatever higher power they believe in. Talk to your higher power daily; God is life, and is everywhere. So talk to God, whatever you perceive him to be, about all of your life. As a child, I was told to pray for others; I now realise that I also have to pray for myself as well. Nobody knows better than God about the obstacles in life. A situation arose when my daughter-in-law was pregnant with twins. Due to complications the doctor gave three possibilities: a one in three chance that one would die; a one in three chance that two would die; and a one in three chance that both would live. For my wife and I, this pregnancy was our first grandchildren. I had no control over the situation. I had a long hard talk with God. I was deep in prayer; I was convinced God was listening. The only way I can explain this is that it was like a power surge in my head. At the end of this talk I said, "Right, that is it. I can do no more, I am leaving it in your hands." The twins were born premature, but perfectly healthy. So, not only did choice theory turn my life around for the good, doors started to open; doors that were always open, but I was blind, and I did not see. Choice theory unlocked my tunnel vision to life; it opened my mind to God and gave me the choice to choose to talk to him together with the freedom to start making better choices that would improve a whole range of things in my life.

Why do we 'behave' the way we do? Behaviour is a word that a large majority of people seldom give a second thought to. If you ask someone, "What is behaviour?", they will say, "Sure everyone knows it is what we do." The reason we behave is to meet our basic needs. As already mentioned, we have five basic needs: survival, love and belonging, fun, freedom, and power. Psychologists recognise that human needs are instinctive, general, and universal. The strength of a person's needs varies dramatically, for example, some people have a small need for power while some have a very high need. As already stated most politicians and performers have a high need for power. A mother or father who spends their life nurturing their family in the home may have a low need for power but a high need for love and belonging. A person with a high freedom-need may find it difficult to work indoors. It can be difficult to have a lasting relationship, if one person has a low need for freedom and the other person a high need. If one or more of our needs is not met; we are frustrated. For example, if a person is hungry, they behave in a way that will satisfy this need. In other words, they will eat and drink to satisfy their need for survival. A person with a high need for freedom will want to go out more often. So our behaviour is everything we do to satisfy what we want at any given moment. We all have experienced saying to ourselves, "I would love to go to town", or "I think I'll go to town." This is one or more of our needs motivating us to choose a behaviour that will satisfy that need or needs. It may be our freedom need, our power need, our fun need, or a combination of all three. But whatever need it is, we behave in order to satisfy that need.

Basic needs do not change; the basic needs of a new-born infant are the same as those of a 20-year-old, a 50; or 90-year-old, but the manner in which they are satisfied – as people grow and mature – differ. Age environment and experience play a large role in determining what satisfies one's individual need. What drives us to meet our needs is what Dr Glasser describes as our 'quality world'. This quality world starts from the time we are born. We hold on to images that are pleasing: images of people, places and things that satisfied us. This type of photographic album which we create in our minds never ends. As we grow, our likes and dislikes change, and as a result, the pictures in our album also change. For example, a young person will have an image in their mind of a certain electronic gadget that they want more than anything. That image will stay in their quality world until they want something completely different. A lot of people have a car in their quality world, some even give them pet names, but as soon as they get a new car, the picture of the old one will fade away. We have images of certain things stored that pleased us, so we find ourselves choosing a particular type of furniture, or a garden swing, or planting a certain tree. Some people might collect old toys, some even pay large amounts of money to have them restored. The image is still in their quality world of a pleasurable experience as a child, and they behave in an attempt to feel some of that childish pleasure. All of this behaviour is influenced by our quality world album; you could say you have been shopping in your quality world store. So, a person's behaviour will be influenced by their quality world pictures. Each person lives their lives through their quality world based on their attempts to satisfy their basic needs.

If we choose to change our belief, we can free ourselves from a lot of misery. Ideas such as, "What choice do I have"; "He or she drives me mad"; "He or she made me do it." Nobody can make you do anything you do not want to do. Making the choice to stop blaming others for a range of unhealthy and unhelpful behaviours will automatically improve a person's well-being. In the knowledge that we are internally motivated, all our behaviour is chosen. All anyone or anything can give us is information; they cannot make us do anything. The pictures in our quality world, based on our attempts to satisfy our basic needs, are what motivates us to behave.

We are continuously confronted with situations which require a choice of behaviour. The behaviours we choose frequently do not satisfy our needs and so result in frustration or an imbalance in our life, thus creating unhappiness. This happens because a place in the brain, which Dr Glasser calls the comparing place, compares, contrasts, and judges what the person has or gets with the quality world pictures in their heads. In other words, their satisfaction from previous choices, which motivated them to behave as they did to satisfy their then needs, based on the pictures in their heads, become frustrated, and found wanting when weighed against their existing quality world pictures thus causing them to frustrate and become unhappy and dissatisfied. In Glasserian psychology terms, their scales go out of balance.

For example, a person searching for something that up until now was always available, chooses to look for a different version of what they wanted in an attempt to satisfy their need. If all efforts fail, they will remain frustrated. When a person is frustrated, they are motivated to behave in order to eliminate their frustration. The behaviour they choose may be a known behaviour or they may choose a new behaviour. Whatever the choice is, it will be that person's best choice to satisfy a need at a particular time. Until the person achieves satisfaction and balance in their life, they will continue to search for a behaviour to satisfy their need or needs.

Our behaviour consists of components, thinking, acting, feeling, and physiology. The strange thing about this is that they all happen at the same time. Thinking, acting, feeling, and physiology – they are four inseparable components that together make up the manner in which we behave. Dr Glasser describes this as total behaviour. All four components work simultaneously, but we have the most direct control over our thinking and acting. Whereas our feelings and physiology are the components that best indicate that our needs are not being met. If our needs are not being met then our scales are out of balance, and we are motivated to choose to change our behaviour to satisfy our unmet needs. This we do by thinking and acting upon reorganised known behaviours, or by creating new ones. An example is, if you are driving a long distance regularly and you are familiar with two directions in reaching your destination, if a tree is blocking one of the directions, you will use your known behaviour, reorganise and take an alternative known route. This type of behaviour is replicated in our daily life in a lot of other situations.

Another example is, take the behaviour of walking; you feel the need to go for a walk and renew energy. Behaviour results from your feeling the need to renew energy so you think about going for a walk. You go for a walk and your behaviour results in your heart and lungs now working at a different rate and you feel satisfied. An easy way to understand how thinking, acting, feeling, and physiology is part of our behaviour is if we consider what happens when we choose to get angry, our body becomes tense, our heart and lungs work at emergency mood, our thinking becomes blurred, and our acting is erratic. It is obvious that our choosing to be angry is not perceived by our quality world as satisfying behaviour. Now this next part is very important as I have just said four things happen when we behave. To restore balance, we need to choose a change of behaviour. To change our feelings of anger and its resulting consequences of tension in our heart and lungs, we must change our thinking and acting, as already stated choosing to change our behaviour changes our feelings and physiology.

As I was writing this, my computer shut down. I used my knowledge of choice theory to deal with this. There was a time my behaviour would have been a combination of a lot of bad language and most likely banging my computer. So, I choose not to react in any negative way, knowing that such behaviour would be pointless, as the only thing I would achieve would be the loss of my peace of mind and the possibility of damaging my computer. So, I put on the kettle to have some tea only to discover that all the power in the house was off. I sat back down to reflect on what I might do while waiting on the power to return. Searching for something positive to do, I realised my books and notebooks were all around the house – the bathroom, the bedroom, the floor – so I spent the next hour collecting, sorting, and finding one particular space for everything. When I finished, I realised the power had returned, and thankfully, I did not choose to overreact.

When people have their basic needs met their satisfaction with life is clearly evident. There is a contentment in a person's face. They are able to deal with everyday problems in a controlled manner. Having a balance between mind and body facilitates this satisfaction. We have all met such people. It is a pleasure to be in their company and if you are lucky enough to spend long periods with such people, it rubs off.

If you are suffering in any way, focus on the way you are behaving, try and visualise your total behaviour. If your doctor cannot find anything wrong with you, examine as best you can, what you are doing. In some cases, a small change in behaviour can make a big difference. For example, you may suffer headaches from stress, choose to change your behaviour, or indeed your lifestyle by slowing down and taking life more leisurely. A small change can make a big difference, say to yourself, "From now on, I am going to slow down I am just going to take life more measured." If you are feeling isolated and lonely, you could choose to talk to your neighbour, or phone someone close to you. I know of situations where people are more than willing to help their neighbours out in anyway but are reluctant to impose in case they may be rejected. With this knowledge of choice theory, you can choose to make better choices to improve your life. You will be amazed how kind and caring people can be.

Our manner of thinking can affect our health. It is advisable to choose to think positively especially about the things you may not find attractive. When you feel you do not like something, choose to see the positive in it. It could be the rain, say, "Well, it will clear the air and water the flora." It could be a neighbour, say, "Well, he or she has a lot on their mind with a troublesome partner and two children to care for." Negative thinking is unhealthy. Negative thoughts stop the flow of the positive thought process and will destroy your creativity; we have the ability to change the way we think. If you have negative thoughts, choose to stop, and reflect; you may have picked up such a habit from being in the company of negative people. We sometimes pick up negative thoughts without realising it. Life is too precious and short to be wasting time preoccupied with negative thoughts; time that could be spent in a more positive productive way. If for some reason, your thoughts are negative, now that you know you can change the way you think, ask God for help to make a choice to change your thinking; this will result in a change of behaviour.

We have all met people who are confident about most things but for some people that is not the case. Not having confidence, we try to protect ourselves as best we can by being cautious. Unfortunately, our mind starts the negative process; this process dampens our confidence. In some cases, we convince ourselves we are not good enough that there is something wrong with us. It is good to remember that we are all God's children. If a person is choosing negative thoughts that person will be unable to enjoy and embrace the world.

Whatever potential the person may have will never be achieved if they continue to choose to think negatively. The negative thinking encourages a person to blame and complain without realising it. Choosing to think positive gives a person freedom. An example would be, if you get a puncture or if you are late for an appointment, an alternative to "Why does it always happen to me?" would be, "Well, that is unfortunate, but things happen. It could be worse; it may have saved a bigger cross." Or an alternative for saying, "I am the unluckiest person you could meet; I have never won anything in my life" could be, "I am very fortunate in life; I am blessed with good health, and I have a loving family around me." The use of bad language automatically puts us in the negative; if you are like me and you sometimes use bad language without realising it, try and stop. Choosing to change your thinking from negative to positive can be achieved remarkably quick. Forgiveness is a gift from God; we sometimes misunderstand the meaning of forgiveness, especially when another person harms you or your family. God has given us this special ability to forgive; we are asked to see the love in all, even the offender.

I would suggest that you use this gift of forgiveness on yourself. It is for you to forgive yourself, to remove all negative thoughts to free your body and soul, to enable you to start living positively again. There is no gain whatsoever in holding resentment; it is a complete waste of a person's time and health. Forgiveness is about freeing oneself from hatred, resentment, jealousy; feelings that stop a person living a happy satisfying life, feelings that in some cases will shorten a person's life. Hatred can eat you up. It can destroy your life and anyone close to you. When you have forgiven yourself, you will feel a freedom; a freedom to live a full and happy satisfying life. This in turn allows you to forgive others. It is normal to feel hurt, but it is unhealthy to hold on to that feeling; holding on to negative feelings is only keeping hatred and evil alive in the world. In a family situation, such emotions can be passed on to children.

Everyday living presents obstacles and difficulties; it is all part of human existence. When a person is born into this world, there is no contract that says welcome to utopia. A lot of people want unrealistic outcomes in life; some people want to be the best soprano in the world, or the best boxer, or the best formula one driver. Only a handful of people achieve this in a generation. Some people spend a lot of time chasing fantasies. If things in your life are reasonably satisfying, yet you may want to improve it, small improvements can be just as satisfying. Choosing acceptance of your situation in life will bring contentment; this in turn gives a person freedom to enjoy life. Most of us are aware that there are people a lot worse off than ourselves. A lot of us, myself included, tend to get sucked into a false type of world; we are brainwashed into a way of life that makes billionaires more billions. A couple of adds come to mind, short term loans, very rich people exploiting the poor, or the new mobile phone.

When you start a relationship with God, you will find material things no longer have the meaning you thought they had. Some people crave for certain things and think that their life will not be complete until they get what they want. It may be a second car, a holiday home, a swimming pool, a luxury holiday, or a bigger house, only to find that after a short time, what they craved for is not making them feel complete. The novelty eventually fades. When we start a relationship with

God, it changes our mindset. We start to see the world with different eyes. We begin to see the beauty in life itself we get energy to explore and discover; we no longer think just about ourselves. Some people may decide to do charity work. Some businesspeople may change their whole approach to the way they do business. Some people just start living. Most of us like nice things, and that is fine if we choose to prioritise the meaningful things in life first. The way to achieving a satisfying life is by making the choice to think for oneself without the influence of the media, to stop and question one's behaviour. It is choosing to ask ourselves, "Have I decided this behaviour, or is it something outside me? Is this really my decision?" If you have a relationship with God then you have a direction; you will begin to see how short and fragile human life is. This will exercise your mind and help you prioritise meaningful aspects of life; resulting in your not craving for the holiday home or the swimming pool, thus making it difficult to be sucked into consumerism. Unlike material things, God's love is not something we start taking for granted. It is not a novelty; it never loses its appeal. To quote Saint Paul,

"*I urge you, then, brothers, remembering the mercies of God, to offer your bodies as a living sacrifice, dedicated and acceptable to God; that is the kind of worship for you, as sensible people. Do not model your behaviour on the contemporary world, but let the renewing of your minds transform you, so that you may discern for yourselves what is the will of God – what is good and acceptable and mature.*" Romans 12: 1–2.

It is advisable to not allow obstacles and life's difficulties dominate your mind; this is not what God wants. Yes, there are problems; yes, there are difficulties, but we must deal with them in such a way that they do not consume us. Problems come in all sizes, almost every problem can be solved provided there is a willingness to do so. Your roof may be leaking, and you have no money to fix it, or you may need a taxi to get to a hospital; there are charities in most places that can help. If you happen to be in financial difficulties, credit unions can work a budget plan for you. In Ireland, we have a facility called Citizens Advice where you can find out all of your entitlements. I would advise anyone not to dwell over a problem and allow it fester and grow. I find when I have a problem, it sometimes helps if I ask myself what would John or Mary do if they had this problem. Trying to visualise how another person would deal with a particular problem can sometimes help. We all see the same problem in a different way. There are some women with large families who amaze people with their coping abilities; how they can deal with all of life's problems, but they do. Why? Because in most cases they choose not to dwell on problems. If we are able-bodied it is healthy to keep ourselves occupied. We sometimes create problems that do not exist. When my children reached an age where they started going out at night alone, the problems I drummed up in my mind are too numerous to mention. I worried about every conceivable outcome which never materialised. So the hard lesson I had learned was, do not worry about something until it happens because there is an endless list of things a person can worry about that will never happen.

We tend to forget that we are dealing with problems all our lives. We have the ability within us as to how we choose to deal with the problem. We cannot allow such things take over our lives. You are special, I am special; we have not been given life to waste it worrying. Choose to deal with situations in a calm and responsible way, and never worry about things that are out of your control. Professional help is available to facilitate people find solutions to their problems; this might be necessary and beneficial in situations where young people are being bullied by parents, older siblings or classmates.

I choose to believe that God has given each person a gift or talent; look within yourself, reflect on what interest you and what you are good at and cultivate it. You may not have the gift to be a concert pianist; your gift may be expressions of love, teaching, organisational skills, a good listener, or a compassionate person. We all have special qualities that God has given us. I would encourage you to first believe in yourself, be confident. Every person is special in God's eyes; from the first breath, you are what God wanted for the world, that special gift of life. We have within us power and ability beyond our imagination, just talk to God, ask for his inspiration and courage, and follow your dream. What I am doing now, writing this book, is as far as I am concerned, an inspiration from God. I had just finished reading a book, and my mind kept wandering, and then in a split second, it was in my mind. Write a book, a combination of the good in choice theory and the good in God. Never in my wildest imagination would I have considered it before that.

"Paul, called by the will of God to be an apostle of Christ Jesus, and Sosthenes, our brother, to the church of God in

Corinth, to those who have been consecrated in Christ Jesus and called to be God's holy people, with all those everywhere who call on the name of our Lord Jesus Christ, their Lord as well as ours. Grace to you and peace from God our Father and the Lord Jesus Christ. I am continually thanking God about you, for the grace of God which you have been given in Christ Jesus; in him you have been richly endowed in every kind of utterance and knowledge; so firmly has witness to Christ taken root in you. And so, you are not lacking in any gift as you wait for our Lord Jesus Christ to be revealed; he will continue to give you strength till the very end, so that you will be irreproachable on the Day of our Lord Jesus Christ. You can rely on God, who has called you to be partners with his Son Jesus Christ our Lord." Paul's First letter to the Corinthians, 1–9.

In Ireland, there are thousands of people doing excellent work in the name of God, I would go so far as saying some of them are walking saints, and I am sure the same can be said all over the world. But there are still, large percentages that go to mass on Sunday who are genuine in their commitment, and for some reason they forget about God until the following Sunday. Looking back at my own behaviour, I would say that I was in that category saying, "That is it for now, until next week, I have done my duty." When you look at how other religions live their belief, they indicate strong conviction in what they believe in. Jews, Muslims, Hindu, Sikhism, and good for them, they are to be admired. Their religion is part of them; it is in most cases, part of their daily life. Catholicism in my opinion, is lagging behind; you could say, we in Ireland, are not taking responsibility for our religion. There appears to be a sort of embarrassment with some people about their belief.

Take Americans, God is part of their vocabulary; God bless America, God given rights, in God we trust, God as judge. This strong belief in my opinion is what has made America great. The pioneers came up against monumental challenges; they asked God for help and guidance and had a strong faith that God would guide them. Against all the odds, they achieved what seemed impossible. One of the problems in Ireland was if you wanted to go to mass or talk to a priest, it involved no effort; we had priests coming out of the woodwork. Their availability was too easy, so we did not appreciate its value. Most things in life that are worthwhile involve some effort. In parts of Africa, people go to extraordinary lengths, walking for hours to participate in mass. For too long now, we left the responsibility of passing on the faith to the priests. Now that priests are few, it is time to take responsibility; families need to take the task of cultivating preserving and passing on their religion seriously. When we start dismissing certain parts such as, reflection during Lent, saying the Rosary daily, in a short time, we will be back to being pagans.

I am aware that a lot of young people are very committed, and doing fantastic work but more needs to be done. There is only so much priests can do. The family unit has suffered badly. The absence of God in the family is increasing. When the family went to mass every Sunday, it had a grounding effect. It allowed people to focus on their principles and direction in life. There is a feeling of belonging being part of a community, young and old have the opportunity to get to know their neighbours. The mass keeps the family unit and the wider Christian family together; it is a celebration they share. Most parents love being part of every aspect of their children maturing, and mass is an integral part of that process. The consequence of missing mass cannot be overstated. In a very short time, the absence of God in a person's life, is and can be alarming. Some people just lose their ability to care for their fellow human beings. They seem to devote all their energy on just themselves. The effects of this can be seen in places throughout the world, in their disrespectful attitudes towards other human beings and towards living creatures and the environment. This behaviour can be witnessed on a daily basis.

Not observing God's guidance from Sunday to Sunday is a big mistake. This is our misfortune; we are missing out on an opportunity to talk to someone who loves us warts and all. We have six days when we could be attentive to his guidance in our life. Think of all the situations a person is presented with in a week. I cannot over emphasise the tremendous contentment and help you can get by just talking to God every day. By saying some small prayer just before you go to sleep is a lovely way to end the day; it draws a peaceful closure to your toil. I was talking to a friend about this Sunday practice, and I mentioned a certain person who attends mass every Sunday, and who for want of a better word is a bit of a character. I am sure there are a lot of us who know similar characters and may question their sincerity. Well, my friend gave me the answer. "Imagine," he said, "what he would be like if he did not go to mass on Sunday." Well that put me back in my box and reminded me of how quick I was to judge. My point is how our relationship with God affects us; it gets our mind and body in harmony it has a soothing calming influence. It is difficult to deny that after celebrating Mass and receiving communion that you do not feel a difference.

The following is an article from the Irish Times 8/6/2019 written by Oliver Callan a writer and satirist, and, as he claims himself, a non-believer 'Don't throw baby Jesus out with the bath water'.

Last August when I was asked to join a panel covering the Pope's visit, I feared I was expected to be the token church bashing gay. I explained that while there was much the catholic church had done wrong, I believe we need to acknowledge the importance of faith to many people. Mass attendances have fallen sharply since the 1990s, and I wonder if that sudden drop in spending 45 minutes a week thinking about life and mortality is linked to increases in mental health problems. With growing antidepressant dependency, a wave of anxiety and high suicide rates, there's a fair argument that we may have a God-shaped hole in our lives. Perhaps we are also letting down young people by being so dismissive of religious practice, and portraying young believers as oddballs, living in the dark outside 'advanced' society. How far can we go in our separation from Catholicism, without losing those virtuous elements, from volunteering to providing a space to think, reflect, grieve? This became the theme of Divorcing God, my documentary about the rise of secularism. I look at the campaign to remove all symbols and signs of the church from State services, to take down statues and change the names of schools and hospitals. In parts of our media, Catholic faith has been declared dead and, along with it, a faith tradition going back thousands of years. The rush to sever all ties feels too extreme and my trip around the country making the programme has confirmed that view. I was born in Our Lady of Lourdes Hospital in Drogheda, founded by the Medical Missionaries of Mary but now entirely owned and run by the state. Although most people in the northeast know it as 'The Lourdes' there are calls to change its name to something secular, a rather brutal effort to erase the heritage and history of a hospital that has served communities since 1957. Since independence from Britain, we have been happy to conserve many symbols of its empire from buildings, post boxes, statues, and coats of arms. The 'royal' prefix remains on prominent institutions with State funding. Swathes of the country kept British names for our streets and squares. Why? Recognition perhaps that our colonial oppressors did some good and an acceptance that its long dominance is an inseparable part of our identity. The tacit independence gained from the Catholic Church over the last three decades ought to be no different. Our young State's period under Vatican control also left a mark on our Irishness. The brand of secularism that seeks to erase and censor it now, risks mimicking the worst traits of the church they're trying to delete. At Presentation Collage Secondary School in Athenry, I found a more grown-up attitude among the teenagers there. Almost none attend Mass on a regular basis, but every hand rose in opposition to removing Catholic symbols, like the school's name, its church window logo, and its motto 'Moladh go deo Le Dia'. Even an atheist pupil said it was important to remember how the school came into being and the legacy of the order led by Nano Nagle. It's a State school now, finally free of religious dominance, but the next generation are wary of ghosting its heritage. Constituency of faithful. In my travels I found that although Mass attendances have fallen, the Catholic Church still has more followers than many of us in media and society acknowledge. From an 81% weekly church-going population in 1990, that figure is now about 30 per cent. So about 1.4 million people still go to Mass every Sunday, a huge constituency of faithful that too many of us pretend doesn't exist. Clearly, these people don't vote according to the wishes of their church on social issues. Perhaps if the judgemental Catholic hierarchy was influenced by its more compassionate congregation, its future would be in better shape. On the other foot, I've found that those embracing the non-religious way are few and struggling. Over 90 per cent of babies born in Ireland are still baptised, even with the lifting of school Baptism barriers. And 11,000 couples get married in a Catholic church every year, almost half of all marriages. Communions and Confirmations continue to be the main milestones in our children's lives, proving that the Catholic tradition matters more to us than we often claim. It's so easy and fashionable to attack the church that even Cabinet Ministers merrily shoot the daft outbursts of bishops like fish in barrels. However, when bereaved, we depend on funeral services and take for granted the parish graveyards that provide a permanent place to grieve. Some 89 per cent of people identified with a religious faith in the last census. We remain religious but how we practise faith has dramatically changed. Those claiming to be non-religious are the fastest growing minority, but they remain a minority at under 10 per cent. Parents going the whole way in not baptising their children nor having them join in other sacraments are still very few, for all the talk of backlash. One parent I met was made so uncomfortable for opting her kids out of sacraments, she once found herself in a hair salon describing a communion day that never happened. When the

Catholic Church was at its worst, it wanted to control, create moral panics, and demonise. At its best, it provided carers, educators and that crucial time and space to think about life's questions. As a non-believer, I fear we will lose something important and good if we charge ahead and throw the baby Jesus out with the bath water.

All my life, I have experienced change, new inventions, different types of music, fashion, and through the majority of this change people maintained high values and respect for oneself and others. In the last couple of years, values and respect by a large number of people has disappeared and has been replaced with a magnitude of unsocial behaviour. Bad behaviour by young people is unacceptable; disrespectful behaviour has become acceptable among some, who have lost respect for themselves and everyone they come in contact with. Behaviour has deteriorated to the extent that employees on public transport are being verbally and physically abused; it has even progressed onto aeroplanes. Crime, such as damage to public and private property, where the taxpayer has to pay is unacceptable.

Why is it? Some of the reasons are alcohol and drugs, or both. Another problem is that some parents are not spending enough quality time with their children. One thing that comes to mind is families not sitting down together for meals regularly. This quality time has always been used for all family members to talk about whatever maybe on their mind. A large number of age groups are eating out now, and a simple thing like this could very well be one of the problems.

Traditional values are being lost; some young people appear to spend their teenage years with an 'I want approach to life'. Values are not important; they are looked upon as natural phenomena. In the space of about ten years, we have turned our back on hundreds of years of culture. Our culture is slowly dying, we are losing our values, and therefore, our identity is in danger, with the possibility of becoming a stand for nothing nation. A 'yes' nation; yes to everything with no regard for our history. People in general appear to be losing that feeling, and sense of belonging to what it is like to be Irish; to serve the common good, and to respect Irish family values, our culture, and our identity. We, now, have started going down a pathway of acceptance without proper reflection, and from a Christian point of view, I feel it is a dangerous path.

"Anyone who wants to become great among you must be your servant, and anyone one who wants to be first among you must be your slave, just as the Son of man came not to be served but to serve, and to give his life as a ransom for many." Matthew: 20: 26–28.

Traditional values and our culture must have a voice; if we turn our back on what our ancestors lived and died for it will be lost forever. We must stand together and be strong, or hundreds of years of nurture and culture will be gone, deleting the past destroys the future. We need to change our mind set. Collective thinking would have a ripple effect so let us start sending out that collective feeling. Imagine a society that is inclusive a society, where people did not have to beg on the street, where children did not have to go hungry, where there was no such thing as homelessness, where the elderly received good medical care. An inclusive society would lessen the need for escapist behaviour A large amount of people who seek escapist behaviour are not meeting their needs; the one need that is most important is that of love and belonging. They need to feel that somebody cares and that they belong in society. Unacceptable behaviour would be reduced dramatically when people start seeing that society cares about them.

We do not have to accept that hundreds of years of family tradition is going down the drain. A major part of family is respect for your elders, and equally and more important respect for oneself. Are we going to replace it with the influence of social media? The poor in general are the people who suffer from lack of respect. Young people need to have self-respect, respect for others, and understand their responsibility as citizens of the state. It is a person's duty to choose behaviour that does not have a negative impact on society.

We must take responsibility. We had a country we were proud of; a nation of people who treasured the land and were the salt of the earth. We are in a place now where there is a danger that sensitivity is being stolen from us, violence has become normalised. The easy way is to do nothing; doing the right thing takes effort we must make the effort. There are many groups up and down the country demanding their rights forgetting that with rights goes responsibility. As a person, I need my rights, the right to my home, my freedom and to live in peace as a human being, and I am sure there are many more like me. If Jesus were living in Ireland today, his teaching would be that we treat one another with respect and justice and live in peace knowing that this is the will of his Father for all humankind. The amount of pain and suffering that criminals have inflicted on innocent people is a national scandal. When it comes to murder, this pain is carried by a second generation and sometimes a third generation. Choosing to condemn criminal behaviour, especially what may now be described as minor, can help. Young people will make mistakes; it is the small mistakes that can lead to bigger ones. Good positive guidance is important in the formative years.

This gift of choice is something we should use wisely; God has given us this freedom to make our own choice. Most of our day-to-day choices are basic but there are times when a choice is significant. It may be in relation to your employment, a temptation to steal. Asking God for direction can help clear your mind. Contemplating on adultery is a significant choice to make. When faced with temptation, prayer might help clear a person's mind. Abortion is a choice that some woman may consider; this can be an extremely difficult time in a person's life. Asking God for help in this difficult time can help a person see more clearly. It can help open up a person's mind to other possibilities and alternatives such as adoption or perhaps the father wants his child or a relative could care for the child. The distress that some fathers experience at such times can get overlooked and forgotten. Prayer can help show us some of the different choices there are. God has blessed women with a very special body that can give birth. Yes, God has given us freedom of choice, and most of us try our best to make the right choices. How do we know what is right? It is within us, our conscious, any time we do something wrong, we know instinctively it does not feel right. Even seasoned criminals will use the phrase "I got away with it" implying, it was not right. Society cannot make up new rights and wrongs just because God's commandments and the natural laws are inconvenient. If a person believes in God, then they must accept that the commandments are there for a reason. Human beings have not changed since Jesus walked this earth; they have the same brains the same needs. God does not live in a time zone; 2000 years ago is now, the same as 2000 years in the future will still be now where God is concerned God is here and now.

External control is a psychology or an approach to living that Dr Glasser talks about extensively. Without realising it, and because it is what we have been accustomed to, and because we consider it to be common sense, many use external control. A person who is being told what to do, at the very least, immediately feels inadequate. This behaviour is hurtful; it instantly removes a person freedom to choose.

A large percentage of people have been telling other people what to do for hundreds of years. People in relationships telling each other what to do; brothers, sisters and parents telling children; grandparents telling grandchildren; religious institutions, governments, schools, workplace managers all telling others what to do. At a particular age, we discover what is right for us. And this is a nice feeling, 'eureka', suddenly life and all it has to offer becomes clear. This is maturity; we start to realise, and feel what we really want and what direction to go in. Thoughts are flooding into our mind. Unfortunately, a lot of people start to think, *if it is right for me, it is right for you*, and they try to impose their ideas on others. Examples, rewarding others to do exam papers for them, influencing younger vulnerable people to steal for them, encouraging their peers to take alcohol or drugs, behaving badly in the company of friends, such as damaging property and not observing the law of the land in the hope that they will impress and that others will copy them. External control is not only psychical and verbal; body language can in some cases be as hurtful and as intimidating. Having the threat of physical force in the form of body language is a silent form of external control.

We do not like to be told what to do, telling people what to do is the foundation of external control. When we are told what to do, we feel threatened. Our freedom to choose is gone. We do not tell our friends what to do, or if we did, we would not have friends. A lot of people in relationships are unhappy for this very reason because one or the other party tells the other what to do. People in a relationship should continually ask themselves, "Will what I am about to do bring me closer to my partner or move us further apart?" Dr Glasser lists seven deadly, or disconnecting habits that we should avoid, in order to create and maintain good relationships. These are criticising, blaming, complaining, nagging, threatening, punishing, rewarding, or bribing to control. These disconnection habits ought to be replaced with the seven connecting habits: listening, respecting, accepting, encouraging, supporting, trusting, and negotiating differences.

I see a similarity in the seven deadly sins. Our pride may make us criticise blame and complain. Our envy, gluttony and wrath may make us nag threaten and punish. Our lust, greed and sloth may make us irresponsible, reward or bribe, and threaten.

The virtues of faith hope and charity would see us listening supporting and encouraging; Prudence, temperance, courage, and justice could see us respecting, accepting, negotiation and trusting.

Whenever a person is exposed to external control over a long period, that person may become anxious frustrated and depressed. This is an unhappy situation, and it is this unhappiness that can trigger a person's creative system, producing many sorts of phobias and health problems. Headaches, fatigue, back pain, lack of concentration, anxiety, lack of self-esteem, not wanting to communicate with others, and agoraphobia are examples of what the creative system can offer in times of stress. When a person persists in keeping another person under their influence with external control behaviour that person may choose to misery or depress.

This behaviour is the controlled person's way of controlling the bully. Because we are internally motivated, choice theory can guide us to a path of internal freedom, we have the ability to change how we think, untapped ability. This change in thinking will open up different possibilities that offer a new way of life; a life free from external control.

Some people practice external control on others in the belief that this behaviour is power. This behaviour, in fact, is feeding the need for power in a misappropriate and confused way. The more success a person has in the use of external control, albeit that person's misguided perception, the more a person will use it. A person who holds this belief mistakenly believes that this is power. This type of power is the result of exposure to external control. True believers of external control are emotionally crippled. They not only bring pain and misery to other people, but they also isolate themselves from possible lifelong friendships, the respect of family, and a contented life.

Social media is excellent in many ways, but as a lot of young people today know, it can be very unsocial or unfriendly. Bullying through this medium has become the choice of some. A person who is at the receiving end can suffer badly, but if they could start the practice of choice theory, along with God's help, they could rise above this poison. If they embrace choice theory, they will be amazed at all the different directions and possibilities that are open to them. It is important that young people start using social media in a responsible way. If a person is being bullied, they should tell the proper authorities.

Choose to think of your mobile number or email address as very personal. You should feel you can trust whoever you give it to. It is inadvisable to put photographs of oneself on social media. You will be admired all the more for not running with the crowd. This medium is unhealthy if overused it could be addictive. Addiction in any form consumes a person's life. It will dictate the number of hours, if any, of personal freedom you might have in your life.

On the matter of depression, some people for a variety of reasons, may choose to stay depressed. Feeling down when you are disappointed about something is fine; it is normal. Choosing to hold on to this feeling for too long is unhealthy. For example, whenever a person is being bullied, they may sometimes choose to be depressed. This choice is an attempt to try and get some control back into their life. In some cases, this can be effective, provided it is only for a short period. It can help manage anger and avoid conflict. Some choose to be depressed in the belief they may receive some form of sympathy. This is their way of bulling the bully, or getting their own way. A person can change difficult situations by making better choices, they can choose to do it with the help of God. The strength a person can get from prayer is one of life's gifts. With this strength a person can begin to see ways of managing a difficult predicament. There is an answer to most problems in life. It is how a person sees the problem. We all have capabilities we are unaware of until we try. By choosing to pray, you can help unlock your capabilities. I would encourage anyone to give it a try; they have nothing to lose.

We have free will; God cannot help anybody unless they ask or look for help. This psychology of choice theory is a big shift in the way a person thinks. This change in the way we deal with people and things is not easy; it takes practice. Some young people may tend to copy certain behaviour from their peers so as to become part of the group. If a young person is the subject of a prank, the one thing that is foremost in that person's mind is why the group behaved in such a manner towards them and this is devastating for that person. The situation with this young person is that they are unable to see that people who are responsible for such pranks have very little going on in their lives and the only satisfaction they get is the reaction of annoyance on the victim. Without a reaction they move on to someone else. Making the decision to choose the psychology of choice theory, the person subjected to the prank or bulling action can choose to ignore this vindictiveness. It is important that they talk about it, and do not hold it in; this will help to remove the stress. There is the danger a young person who finds themselves a victim of a prolonged campaign of bullying may choose strange behaviours. The distress that a person feels could be magnified unrealistically to a point where the person, in extreme cases, can see no other behavioural solution to their problem than that of suicide. This consequence being the result of what some inconsiderate person put on social media. Choosing to change one's way of perceiving things will not happen overnight, but with practice and God's help it can be done.

At any time, all anyone or anything can give us is information. I can choose to get upset or I can choose to remain calm. So, the key word is information; one can choose to react or not. We may ignore information. Periodically, it may be something our parents said. It could be a news flash on television; this may be relevant to thousands of other people but not to you or me, so you choose to ignore it. We choose the information we want, no matter how significant or insignificant the information is. If we decide it is of no importance to us, we just ignore it. When a person hears bad news that includes a familiar name alarm bells go off in that person's head; a dark cloud descends and the person is consumed with panic, and maybe unable to make any positive decisions. In such situations, it is important to step back, take time out, and calm down. These situations are never as catastrophic as they may appear. The news may be magnified or out of context. If in the case of slander by an unknown person, such news would not be as devastating. So, news is what it is, just news. Words are just words; they may be ugly words, but most of the time the information publicised maybe a collection of lies. Words cannot harm you unless you choose to allow your mind to dwell on such a concoction of slander. In times of stress, there is a greater possibility of making a wrong choice. Whatever the problem is, try and see it for what it is, just another one of life's situations. Choose to take control of the situation, your approach will best help you deal with this; a positive attitude about oneself is paramount. You are a very special individual in this world; people love you and you can choose to rise above this.

Our journey through life has no blueprint. Life is not the same for everyone. We are not all equal; no one person can do everything. Had I a choice, I would have chosen to be six foot two and a singer in a rock band but that was not to be. Life is a mixture of ups and downs, and most of the time, it is fine. Each event will pass, believe me, like all of life's other situations, it will become a distant memory. Think back to when you were a child; you may have had disputes with other children, there may have been times when you were upset or crying, or some other situations that upset you, but you got up, brushed yourself off and got on with life. I am not trying to diminish the severity of any situation by comparing it with, what happened when you were a child. I am trying to point out that we have within us the creative ability to solve problems. Professionals are able to facilitate and enable people to come up with plans to solve their problems and help them to choose to live happy satisfied and fulfilled lives. The professional knows we have the ability within us; all they do is help us discover the way and the means. What seems to be devastating can be overcome with the right choice. When a person's needs are not being met, they can choose to panic and in seeking to satisfy their wants, they choose crazy behaviours. They are unable to see clearly, and usually what happens is they start to exaggerate and become confused. Whatever behaviour you choose, it is your personal choice. It may not seem to be if you are panicking. People have nothing to lose by giving choice theory or Glasserian psychology a chance; there are no side effects.

Young people are influenced by a variety of things. Television is up there as one of the tops. Television producers and film producers have been using professional psychologist since they first started making films, and they know exactly how to push your buttons. Millions are spent in the making of programs, especially the ads, most of what you see bears no resemblance to reality. The shows that are called reality, go to great lengths to engage people who do not look like your average person. Some vulnerable young people want to model themselves on what they see on television and so go on diets, join a gym, or buy new clothes. Such people may believe that they have the right to criticise others because of how they look. They have decided what is fashionable, because they have been influenced by something they have seen on some type of media. One of the most destructive things anyone can do is criticise another. Unfortunately, a small percentage of people will zoom in on anyone who shows a weakness. Once again, a person needs to choose to rise above this destructive and negative behaviour. Look inside yourself for the strength, choose not to let this interfere with your future and what it may hold. Good choices and the incredible power of God will enable one to overcome all adversities.

There is a lot of pressure on young people regarding image. Image is superficial; you are what God has made. Accept your image, love yourself as already stated each person is unique. Life is what it is, some of us are big, some are thin, some very tall, some not so tall. We come in all shapes and sizes. Provided there is no medical problem, just thank God for this opportunity to embrace life. Some food today maybe unhealthy; we have a responsibility to ourselves to eat healthily. If you start getting negative ideas about looks, then negative thoughts magnify in your mind, this is very unhealthy. Looks have a short window; they do not last as the saying goes "Looks are only skin deep." What is attractive about a person, is, firstly their confidence; be confident, each and every one of us are special. Choose to dismiss any negative thoughts. Talk to God to empower you.

"Ask, and it will be given you; search, and you will find; knock, and the door will be opened to you." Matthew 7:7.

With this confidence, your personality will shine. It is not your hair or your feet that are attractive; it is all of you, every little, tiny bit of you. Each person is special. No two people are the same; there is something very attractive in you, the person, and that lasts forever. Prayer will help restore confidence. Temptations are all around us. At a young age, curiosity is understandable. In most cases, if something is not right, our intuition tells us that it just does not feel right; this is our built-in warning device. Sometimes when temptation raises its ugly head, making the right choice can be difficult if you are with a group of friends. Be strong, resist temptation, if your friends look down on you, then calling them friends maybe stretching it. Friends may not always remain friends, but you have to deal with the consequences of bad choices. It is at times like this that our higher power shines, just pray and as sure as day follows night you will make the right choice. We see and hear on news channels every day about bad behaviour; behaviour that could be avoided had people paused and reflected.

We cannot change another person. Understanding this is important especially when a young relationship ends. Our minds are personal to each one of us; how one person perceives something can vary dramatically to what the other person perceives. When two people are in a relationship one person may have a picture in their quality world of a long and lasting future with that person. The other person may have a picture in their quality world of travelling around the world for the sheer excitement of it or to gain a better understanding and appreciation of other cultures. We all wonder at certain things in life; why do people do what they do. Why do some people become doctors, why do some people stay single, why do some people not want children as part of their relationship with another person, why do some people prefer to live in a camper van alone? Each person chooses to start their life with likes and dislikes; as they grow and mature, they build an album of images in their mind. This becomes that person's quality world. So, when that person matures, that person has certain things etched in their mind. They may not like to live in a city. They may not like responsibility. They may not like work. There will be a large amount of food they do not like. We use words like, peculiar habits, unusual, in order to describe people that some of us think are different. We all have a different blueprint in our mind that has been building up over time of what makes us feel good. When there is a decision to be made between two people, a suggestion from one person may very well be dismissed. That suggestion is how that person perceives the situation. The other person, perception of the situation may be different. For example: one person may suggest going bowling, and the other person may say, "I was thinking of going swimming." Or one person may say, "Let's go to the cinema", and the other person may say, "No, I want to watch a football match on television." Our wants and needs differ, so thinking you can change a person is futile, and trying to is external control on your part and could result in ending a relationship.

If a relationship ends, it is advisable to reflect on what you have learned. It may be necessary to choose a behaviour that would bring satisfaction and fulfilment in your life to fill the void resulting from the broken relationship. Talk to your higher power and choose to try your best not to feel sorry for yourself. A small amount of self-pity is acceptable; choose behaviours that will restore happiness contentment and balance to your life. This is an extremely difficult time in a person's life, but it's a part of life. Some young people think it is the end of the world if a relationship breaks down. A person in this situation needs to be helped to understand that thousands of relationships breakdown every day. This emptiness will pass, new and exciting things will enter that person's life. This is not the time to make rash decisions, but the time to choose healthy distractions.

Our creative system is a wonderful part of our behavioural system. We do a lot of things in our daily life without giving it much thought. That is because what we are doing is repeating behaviours – cleaning our teeth, putting the key in the door – they are organised behaviours. Our needs activate our creative system. The eight o'clock bus for work is never on time, so our creativity offers us an alternative, get the seven thirty bus. Now our behaviour has to change in order to get the seven thirty bus, we get up earlier and leave earlier. This change is reorganised behaviour, and we do this for most of our lives. Because of a pandemic, people are unable to travel to work. Our creativity comes up with ways that may help; Zoom and working from home are examples. Our behaviour has two parts. One part contains our familiar organised behaviour. The other part, which is the source of our creativity, contains the building blocks of all behaviours in a constant state of reorganisation.

When a relationship breaks down, and the need for love and belonging is strong sometimes the person comes up with crazy behavioural solutions. The person may create within themselves unfavourable opinions of themselves, for example, imagining they are unattractive. It is like an alarm going off; we are not meeting our quality world picture of love and belonging. The creative system has no idea what to do. All it knows is that its quality world picture of love and belonging is not being met, and so it offers alternative behaviours: I am too fat so I will diet, I am too thin so I will eat more. No matter what alternative behaviour you choose, it is you alone that is choosing it. Our creative system is not a separate part of our body. It is part of us, and therefore, whatever behaviour we choose is our personal choice. Your creative system can come up with new behaviours. Making choices can be difficult but it is our choice to act or not. Our creative system is part of our behavioural system, and any behaviour is total, consisting of feeling, physiology, thinking and acting. But the thoughts that fill our mind in times of despair are coming from our comparative system in an attempt to prompt the creative system to find a behavioural solution in order to restore balance. You may choose a crazy behaviour in an attempt to get balance restored. This can be confusing, and a lot of the time could be dangerous. Your creative system is trying to help by offering you all sorts of ideas. The immediate aftermath of a breakup can be very difficult; time is needed and choosing positive healthy reorganised behaviours is best.

The positive side of our creative system is that life would be meaningless without it. We have a lot of talent shows that run for several weeks, and each week the contestants come up with new and better performances. The people who enter talent shows work very hard trying to achieve a high standard in an attempt to win. This involves a lot of practice, and generally results in great improvement. This improvement gives the contestants a belief that more improvement is possible, so they search for more creative ways. A combination of factors is happening here. It could be a high need for power that motivates the creative system. It may be a need for power and fun, or power, fun, love and belonging. The creative part of the brain offers them reorganised behaviours, where they choose what they perceive to be best for them. The reorganised behaviour needs to be put into effect in the real world and then perceived and evaluated as satisfying.

A large number of people today are suffering with what they believe to be mental illness. There is no pathology, however, to diagnose mental illness. So if there is no pathology to prove or suggest that you are mentally ill, a more valid explanation could be that you are unhappy. You may have symptoms such as anxiety, depression, pain, and anger; your symptoms may be a way of expressing your unhappiness. Relationships play a major role in a person's well-being. This applies to all the important people that are part of a person's life: husband, wife, partner, children, friends, the boss, work colleagues, and neighbours. When a person has good relationships with the important people in their life and their community, they feel good about themselves. A bad relationship distracts a person. It will play on their mind because the natural balance between mind and body is strained. A person can become so consumed over a bad relationship that living a normal life is impossible, resulting in bad health. Paying attention to our loved ones listening to their concerns and spending time with them when needed can only help to nurture a relationship. Without realising it, we sometimes take a good relationship for granted; by choosing to work at maintaining a good relationship we will achieve personal satisfaction. If you find you are feeling uncomfortable because of a bad relationship, perhaps you may choose to improve it. This can be achieved by focusing on the connecting habit; helping your partner in the home, choosing not to complain to your child or children, choosing not to resent the boss, choosing to live, and let live regarding neighbours; forgiveness or a kind word can go a long way.

In Dr Glasser's book, 'WARNING: Psychiatry Can Be Hazardous to Your Mental Health', the foreword is written by an Irishman, Terry Lynch. Dr Lynch realised from reading Dr Glasser's book that his medical training in the area of mental health had been hugely deficient, so he took time out from his medical practice to train in psychotherapy. His further studies culminated in the publication of his book, 'Beyond Prozac Healing Mental Health Suffering Without Drugs'.

Dr Glasser in his book, 'Warning', takes an in depth look at how unhappiness can be misdiagnosed as mental illness. The supposed mental illness becomes the focus of attention, and the underlying human issues go unnoticed and unresolved. A lot of the problems are not mental illness, rather loneliness, isolation, and unhappiness. When you are unhappy, you are not as mentally healthy as you would like to be, but you are not mentally ill. Dr Glasser's suggests perhaps small groups of five to fifteen under the guidance of a choice theorist with the objective of studding choice theory and putting it in to practice. Embracing choice theory is the key to happiness; understanding your needs, with the realisation that the only person you can control is yourself, and the removal of external control from your live. The people in the focus group are not there pacifically to share extensively about their past or present unhappiness. For example, how much trouble they are having getting along with a spouse, parent, child, or boss, or about how much pain they are suffering or how unfair life has been to you. They are interested in hearing about how to apply the choice theory ideas of Glasser to their present problems, and in helping them to learn how to do this more effectively as the group continues to meet. The book, 'Warning', is an attempt to teach people how to help themselves or an unhappy member of the family. If you are reading this and feeling unhappy and would like to help yourself, the very fact that they are reading is evidence enough of their ability to help yourself. Look at how you have been behaving. Have you, without realising, made choices that perhaps you might change. If so, talk to your higher power; ask for strength to help you make better choices. Your higher power can help lift you out of whatever situation you are in.

When a person is unhappy, some of the choices they make, create a lot of pain. And the only person that can feel the full extent of the pain is that person. In some relationships, a person may make a choice out of anger in an attempt to get some control. An example would be, "If I don't get what I want, I am going to make things difficult for you." So you decide you are not going to the birthday party; something you both had agreed on. This choice will make you feel bad, especially if your partner goes, and you find out later how good the party was. You are unable to feel happy when you are feeling bad. What is happening here is, indirectly, you are choosing to give another person control over your happiness, all because of a bad choice. You are choosing your misery. Disagreements in relationships happen, not choosing to reach a compromise is unhealthy. It will serve no purpose; nobody wins and at least one person is left frustrated. Most of the time disagreements are over relatively simple things such as where to go on a night out, what colour are we going to paint the kitchen, should we buy a new television, I want to watch a certain programme. In the broad scheme of things, not to compromise on such inconsequential things is unhelpful and will not make for a good relationship.

When relationships start to break down, and the couple still love each other, and would like a loving atmosphere back, understanding each other's basic needs and quality world is extremely helpful. When each person still holds love for the other, a picture of that person will be in their quality world. If you want the relationship to last, the picture needs to remain. The use of the deadly habits will start to fade the picture. Dr Glasser suggests what he calls the 'solving circle' when there are problems in a relationship. It helps to draw an imaginary circle on the floor. For example, in the situation of a marriage, both you and your partner take chairs and enter the circle. There are three entities in the solving circle: the wife, the husband and the marriage itself. Recognise that you both have strong positions based on the differences in the strength of your needs, but these positions are not so strong that you are unwilling to enter the solving circle. What you are agreeing to when you enter the circle is that the marriage takes precedence over what each of you wants as individuals. Both of you also know choice theory. You know that if you try to force the other, it is likely that the weaker person may feel uncomfortable or will decide to step out of the circle. This is no different for people who are not married and share a life together; working at keeping the relationship is paramount if both still love each other.

Maintaining a relationship can be difficult. In his book, 'Staying Together', Glasser talks about how we respond when a relationship is going downhill. In our mind, it is always someone else, not us, who is at fault. For example, many times in our marriages, we feel angry or depressed and, not knowing choice theory, we don't even consider the possibility that we are choosing to feel upset. We think it is happening to us because of what someone else is doing or failing to do. Better choices are almost always available. An example would be, you get up late for work and you are unable to find your clean shirt or that favourite tie you were going to wear. Starting to stress, you get angry and proceed to blame and complain at your partner. This behaviour will not help a relationship. By making better choices, you can avoid getting stressed and blaming others, for example, leaving your clothes ready before you go to bed. Some people, without knowing choice theory, would deal with such a situation in a calm reasonable way. If you take five or ten minutes to get your clothes ready before going to bed, you can avoid being frustrated and picking on your partner. If you find yourself feeling like blaming your partner on something, stop and consider the possibility that you may be wrong. In most cases, you will find that 90% of the time your partner had no input or control over your affairs. When you receive a large bill for electricity, you may choose to be depressed or angry and blame your partner for using excessive amounts. You may be right, or you may not. By choosing this immediate approach, you will more than likely create friction between yourself and your partner. You could choose to remain calm and say, "The electricity bill seems very big. What can we do about it? I wonder have they made a mistake or maybe we have used more because of the cold weather?" In relationships, a person can sometimes, without realising it, take their partner for granted; good choices in a relationship helps everybody.

It may be difficult to remain happy in a long-term relationship, In America, the following is a quote from 'Secrets of Happy Couples' by Kim Olver, "It took two years of concentrated effort to find one hundred happy, satisfied couples…who had been together at least ten years and who were willing to take my anonymous online survey about their relationship as part of the research for my book." Keeping a good long-term relationship can be difficult if not impossible. If, for example, external control is part of that relationship, this will destroy any relationship. Or the wants of each person differ completely; one person may want to party most of the time, and the other may not. Responsibility is another reason for breakups; one or both not ready or prepared to take responsibility. One person may want a joint bank account, and the other may want to keep their own personal account. The realisation that their pay cheque is no longer theirs alone, some people may find it difficult. All over the world, people just walk away from relationships for all sorts of reasons. Our wishes and aspirations of 'happy ever after' can be disappointing. When we learn the choice theory axiom – *the only person we can control is ourselves* – we gain a sense of control over our lives, which feels very good. It is this sense of control – over ourselves, not over others – that gives choice theory psychology its name.

Choosing not to be depressed when there are problems in a relationship is not easy. Choosing to be depressed is something everybody has learned from a very young age, and most of the time it gets results. Depressing can be a controlling behaviour? Depression can be a controlling behaviour or a cry for help or sympathy; the results of which are very painful because depressed people isolate themselves. In what way? Isolating themselves. Making better choices takes effort; you have to work at it at the start, and gradually it gets easier. If we change the description of our feelings, by avoiding using adjectives and nouns to using verbs, for example, "I am feeling depressed," to "I am choosing to be depressed" or "I am depressed"; it can show that better choices of behaviour are possible and brings a completely different meaning to what seemed to be insurmountable.

Relationships are a crucial part of survival; humans need relationships. They need to communicate with each other. Relationships are part of every aspect of human beings' lives. From the cradle to the grave, human beings encounter situations that compel them to form some sort of a relationship. The behavioural evolution that human beings have reached makes it almost impossible to go through life without forming a relationship; to such an extent that life without contact with others is practically impossible and would be most likely unbearable. From the time a person is born, a relationship is needed, otherwise a person would most likely die. In the majority of cases, the child has a relationship with the parents, predominately with the mother. This nurture is satisfying and meeting the needs of the child, especially the need for love and belonging. As the child grows, relationships will be formed with siblings and friends. The desire to communicate is so powerful that in order to satisfy this desire, a person forms relationship with others. People need to share their thoughts and feelings with someone they like; this is a form of life therapy.

Many people fear or are anxious about certain things. Most people who suffer with anxiety or phobia will say, "Sure, I know it does not make sense." Some of our fears have been picked up perhaps from a parent who, for example, may have had a fear of dogs, or a fear of lifts. Fearful thoughts, over time, get grounded in us. A solution may be to choose to think positive, saying to yourself, "My fear is unrealistic. From now on, I am choosing different thoughts." If perhaps something happened in the past that gave you reason to be fearful, it is unfortunate, but whatever happened in the past, is in the past, we cannot change the past; leave the past where it belongs. Choosing to deal with the present makes one positive decision now. Start with something small and work on it; this will build your confidence and you will go from strength to strength. Do not worry or burden yourself with the future most things usually have a way of working out. The future is something of a mystery,

"So do not worry about tomorrow: tomorrow will take care of itself. Each day has enough trouble of its own." Matthew: 6: 34.

What you can do is make a plan and implement it. Look at ways, small to begin with, just small behavioural changes; slowly at first and along with the help of your higher power, you will overcome most problems. For example, if you have a fear of lifts, get a friend to hold open the doors, walk in and out a couple of times. Do this every day and slowly the fear will pass; you are not going to die. If possible, it is most important to walk outdoors every day for at least 40 minutes. When on occasion, you have important decisions to make, your reasoning may conflict with your choices. The practice of mindfulness is very good; when you get yourself in a state of mindfulness your mind becomes very clear, and it is here you can take full advantage of choice theory. Then in this relaxed state you can see more clearly the best choice for you together with, better choices for other aspects of your life.

In Dr Glasser's book, 'Fibromyalgia: Hope from a Completely New Perspective', the approach is neither medical nor psychiatric; it is strictly educational. Dr Glasser discovered that in America, millions of people, mostly middle and upper-middle-class Caucasian women, suffer from fibromyalgia. This is, according to Dr Glasser, an unwanted part of an ineffective behaviour you are presently choosing, as you try to deal with your unhappiness. With fibromyalgia, your physiology almost always gets involved. The abdominal bloating, diarrhoea, bladder irritation, and fatigue that accompany your muscle pain are the physiological components. Unhappiness affects people differently. It appears the happier you were, the more unhappy you will be when things in your quality world are not going to plan. Our genetic needs will not allow us to accept long-term need frustration without letting us know about it through our feelings and physiology. Fibromyalgics are 90% women, very capable highly motivated women, with high expectations of themselves and others; women who hold responsible demanding jobs, while looking after children and a home. Such women are usually very creative, great planners, problem solvers, ability to deal with a host of situations undeterred but when their quality world pictures are not being met, their creative system kicks in. Without realising it, the strength of their need or needs have put pictures into their quality world that are unachievable; their expectations of themselves, and others, are too high. With this disappointment of not being able to meet their quality world pictures, the creative system reacts in its inability to create a satisfying behaviour. The creative system is just reacting to the person's total behaviour, in this case, most likely, the thinking component. A creative system has no morality. It cannot distinguish between good and bad options. Pain, in some form or another, is a great distraction. It helps the mind deal with what the person perceived to be disappointment. What the person needs to do is to start making better choices. Lowering their expectations would be a good place to start. Begin by changing their quality world pictures, remove unrealistic ones, and with the help of their higher power, they can find satisfying behaviours. It is important to be aware of the fact that no person can change another person, but they can facilitate them look for or search for a solution. They could start changing the way they were thinking and think of better choices they might make. When a person starts making satisfying choices, their behavioural change will lower the frustration, and this in turn, restores balance to the system.

It is important that employees have a good relationship in the workplace. If they are not comfortable at work, they are not meeting their needs. Because of this they, will be frustrated. We all need to experience a certain amount of fun, freedom, and power at work. If this is not the case, one will feel frustrated, and their scales will be out of balance because of the needs not being met. This frustration will waste energy; the quality of work will suffer. Some people may bring their frustration home; others may turn to alcohol or some other drug. In his book, 'The Choice Theory Manager', Dr Glasser is talking to managers. He explains how the quality of work improves in every situation when people are meeting their needs. This happens when people are listened to, when they are given responsibility, when they feel they are part of a business, and when they can see a future for themselves in the company. Glasser lists five conditions for work location quality. The work environment must be warm and supportive; since quality is always useful, workers should only be asked to do useful work and should be encouraged to contribute to the usefulness of what is being done; workers are asked to do the best they can do; from the time workers are hired, lead managers will guide the process of helping them learn to continually evaluate their work; then, based on this ongoing self-evaluation, lead managers will encourage workers to improve the quality of what they do. Quality work always feels good and therefor is personally satisfying.

Each person's perception of the real world differs. In general, we agree on basic things such as time and weather; most people in Ireland do not like the rain. Though there may be a small number who do like rain but that is where it ends. One might consider three people out walking. They stop at a derelict site with a broken-down garage on it. The perception one person may get, might be, *I could start a car wash business here*; another person may think, *this would make a great storage unit for me*; another person may think, *that's disgraceful you would think the authorities would clean that up.* The derelict site was in the real world. What we perceive is our personal perceived world. Our evaluating system is the adjudicator. Perception is a process by which people regard, analyse, retrieve, and react to any kind of information from the environment or real world; our valuing system or quality world determines its usefulness for any individual when placed on the valuing scales. Values that are perceived by the senses are determined by the person's needs and quality world picture. Perceptions are our inner reality. Our senses perceive a particular image, and our perception creates a reality based on our evaluation.

From the time we are born, we try things out in order to see how we feel about them. This happens in the 'real world'. As children mature to adulthood, they will start exploring, seeing, feeling, tasting, smelling, hearing. Whatever is pleasing will go into their photographic album, their quality world. They may try eating onions and find they do not like them, or they may try chocolate, and find they like it. This process never stops, and it is from this process that we stockpile a wealth of knowledge. Everything that pleases us will go into our quality world. As we mature, we behave to meet a need from a picture in our quality world. We behave in the real world to satisfy a need. From the first pleasurable experience the child received from crawling on the floor, the child will cry to be put down on the floor. This good feeling was in the child's quality world from a previous behaviour. Now the fun and freedom needs are motivating the child to cry in order to satisfy again that need or needs and feel good again from the behaviour of crawling. The feedback the child gets goes through a type of filter called a valuing filter and from there to a comparing place in the brain. In this comparing place, there is what choice theory psychologist call a type of weighing scales. How these weighing scales are balanced determines the level of the child's satisfaction. In other words, happiness or unhappiness. In the case of the child crawling, if the experience is similar to the outcome of their previous behaviour, then the child feels good and gets a positive feeling. So the picture they had in their quality world is being met, and the child's weighing scales are in balance; their mind and body are in harmony. If the scales are out of balance, in other words, if the child is not happy and satisfied and is not having their need met, perhaps the child found the next crawling experience unpleasant because the floor surface was different from the first experience. Now a different behaviour is created, and this will continue until the child's needs are met.

Relationships as already mentioned cover a wide range, and marriage is a big decision in a person's life. To get married and have children is a choice most people make. To bring new life into the world is to fulfil God's plan. To populate the earth, God has given us the joy of sex. Choosing to marry is something we must consider very carefully; this commitment is a wonderful thing and blessed by God and contributes greatly to our happiness and fulfilment in life. We choose a life partner with the intention and hope of enjoying a happy satisfying and gratifying life together. Our need for love and belonging pushes us to form relationships. A marriage involves daily commitment; we marry for love or perhaps, think we do. Infatuation feels like love, but it is not and can fade. Marriage is a vocation, and it is only love that will bond this union; to marry is to become 'one flesh.' Marriage is a gift from God, blessed by the Sacrament of

Marriage. When choosing a partner for marriage, it would be advisable to look closely at each other's needs. When a young person is in love, or thinks they are in love, they are unable to see clearly. One person may be in love and the other may not, or it may not be love but infatuation. Looking at each other's needs will help compatibility. For example, if you are a very timid person, and your partner is an adrenaline junkie, this may not be a good match. You may have been attracted to your partner because he or she was exciting, always active, never staying in the one place very long, having to go to different locations regularly. If you are a quite timid person, this behaviour from your partner, that could last a lifetime, may not make a happy marriage. The old adage 'opposites attract' is not always the case. At times, it may be just infatuation, and if so, this could be disastrous for marriage. Couples who share a high need for love and a low need for power tend to be happier together. Couples who share a high need for power and a low need for love will spend a lot of their time bickering about who is in charge and who is right. Life in general has its ups and downs. When you are single, you deal with your individual problems; a married life is totally different. No two people think the same. We are all different, plus the added fact that the wants and needs of males and females differ. A lot of males like gadgets; a lot of females like clothes. Having to compromise is an integral part of marriage, which is why love is so important.

"Love is patient, love bears all things, love is generous, love will see you through." 1 Corinthian 13–4.

Love should come natural, not based on what he or she does for you. If you love a person for what they do for you, that sort of love will not last if they stop doing it. An example could be a person drives me wherever I want to go, and he insists on paying for all my clothes; or she washes and irons all my clothes and she is always buying me presents. What might become of my love for that person if their services stop. Love never seeks its own advantage; you love a person faults and all. For example: a man may think his intended wife is untidy, or a woman may think her intended husband is untidy; they may be right, or they may be wrong. If perhaps one is right that is the way the person is. Will you stop loving that person after the honeymoon because they are untidy; love is unconditional. Here I am reminded of the saying, "You can't live on love." I would argue when two people are giving themselves to each other in love. They are able to achieve some remarkable outcomes. The dynamic that surrounds them is inspiring.

The one thing that is guaranteed to destroy a marriage is external control. When one or both start criticising, complaining, or blaming the other, this is what destroys all marriages. Examples of such behaviour might be; "You are late home from work. It's too late now for me to go to the football match. You knew I had to go at seven. I am sick and tired of you coming home late from work"; "You always embarrass me when we are out with friends. You never make conversation with anyone. You make no effort. I don't know why I married you"; "No matter what I do, you always find fault with it. I can't do anything right." They are just a small sample of the deadly or destructive habits, nagging, threatening, punishing, and bribing are others. There are more ways to use external control but if couples can stop using the seven deadly or destructive habits and replace them with caring or connecting habits, the marriage can and will improve significantly. Listening to what your partner is saying is most important; a person knows if they are being listened to. What may seem minor to one, can be major to another and therefore by listening, hearing, and talking one can reduce the other person's anxiety. An example might be a school report; one parent or guardian is stressed out over it and the other is not overly worried. Talking about this in a calm supporting way and listening to the concerns of the other will in most cases find answers and resolve things.

Arguments in marriages are generally over silly things: "What's for dinner?"; "I cleaned up yesterday"; "I'm not going to that wedding"; "I'm fed-up washing after you"; "Why can't we have a big car like our neighbour next door?" If, for example, things are not going right for you, it could be the result of a number of perceived negative things happening such as, you did not get that promotion you were expecting; the car broke down on the way home; the bank rings you about your overdraft; you end up going to three shops before you get the product you want. Now it is very easy for a partner to start the blame game. If a partner chooses, they can find a million different reasons to pick an argument with the other partner. Choosing to get upset and argue with your partner will not undo any unfortunate happenings. Choosing to argue with someone who had no input or control over what just happened is unhelpful. It is normal and healthy to talk and share about each other's ups and downs in a respectful way. When the honeymoon is over, it is very easy to become a small bit forgetful of each other's needs. It is important that you continue making the effort to be supportive, respecting and accepting each other's views. By supporting, in good and bad times, accepting this person regardless, respecting and trusting one another through life. Each person can have contentment. Each of us are aware of behaviour that could be improved on by taking time to reflect we have the ability to enhance each other's lives.

For those who believe in marriage, it is helpful to include God in sharing the good and the bad times. When you include God in the marriage on a daily basis life, it can have more meaning and be more pleasurable, and you can be better able to deal with the challenges along the way. Hopefully, the gift of new life will be given to the couple. The new-born is the result of mutual love; this is a wonderful time for the couple and a time to rejoice.

"Let faithful love and constancy never leave you: tie them around your neck, write them on the tablet of your heart. Thus you will find favour and success in the sight of God and of people." The Proverbs 3: 1–4.

Dr Glasser has helped millions of people around the world, this booklet is a marriage of Choice theory and your Higher Power. I hope and pray, you the reader, find something in it, to help you take control of your life, and with the help of your higher power, find your way out of whatever pain or unsatisfying circumstances you may be in.

The ten axioms of choice theory are:

1. The only person whose behaviour we can control is our own.
2. All we can give another person is information.
3. All long-lasting psychological problems are relationship problems.
4. The problem is always part of our present life.
5. What happened in the past has everything to do with what we are today, but we can only satisfy our basic needs right now and plan to continue satisfying them in the future.
6. We can only satisfy our needs by satisfying the pictures in our quality world.
7. All we do is behave.
8. All behaviour is total behaviour and is made up of four components: acting, thinking, feeling, and physiology.
9. All total behaviour is chosen, but we only have direct control over the acting and thinking components.
10. We can only control our feeling and physiology indirectly through how we choose to act and think.
11. All total behaviour is designated by verbs and named by the part that is the most recognisable.